RUSKIN BOND

PENGUIN

VIKING

An imprint of Penguin Random House

VIKING

USA | Canada | UK | Ireland | Australia
New Zealand | India | South Africa | China | Singapore

Viking is part of the Penguin Random House group of companies
whose addresses can be found at global.penguinrandomhouse.com

Published by Penguin Random House India Pvt. Ltd
4th Floor, Capital Tower 1, MG Road,
Gurugram 122 002, Haryana, India

Penguin
Random House
India

First published in Viking by Penguin Random House India 2020
This edition published in 2024

11 10 9

The views and opinions expressed in this book are the author's own and the
facts are as reported by him which have been verified to the extent possible,
and the publishers are not in any way liable for the same.

ISBN 9780670093816

Book design and illustrations by Shipra Bharati
Printed at Thomson Press India Ltd, New Delhi

www.penguin.co.in

Introduction

As a small boy I liked to make lists—lists of books I had read, films I had seen (casts included), flowers I had liked, birds I had noticed (and if I didn't know their names I made them up), favourite songs, singers, even colours that appealed to me.

Natural colours—the colour of the sky, the sea, the good earth, all growing things. My favourite colour is purple and I do most of my writing with a purple gel-pen! Sounds and colours go into my stories and poems.

As I grew older, I began to make lists of interesting and helpful thoughts and observations, words of comfort and friendly advice—advice to myself as I was often in need of it, and advice to friends and readers who might have been going through a difficult time. These went to several 'little books' consisting of words of love, courage, compassion, joy and good feelings in general, all coming together to create a gentle philosophy of life.

These are words to live by, and over the years they have continuously helped me. If they can help you too, dear reader, this little book would have served a good purpose.

My thanks to Premanka Goswami of Penguin Random House India for helping me in making this selection from my diaries and purple notebooks.

Ruskin Bond

1 January, 2020

Some people are always
COMPLAINING
because roses have
THORNS.

Let us be
GRATEFUL
that thorns have
ROSES.

today, there are
many more conflicts
all over the world,
and they appear to be
building up into a
major conflagration.

but when a
plain white butterfly
appeared on my
window sill,
heralding the summer,
I had to admit
that there is still
some beauty in the world.

Don't be depressed
by your surroundings.
That pebble at your feet
has as much beauty
as any great work of

I am watching stars
from my window...
I'm aware of
belonging to the

UNIVERSE

RATHER THAN
JUST ONE CORNER
OF THE EARTH.

Go and
do things.

You are bound
to succeed in
some of them.

*This little story
is true
in every respect.*

HISTORY
only tells us about the
GREAT ONES
who left their footprints
on the sands of time.

Dhuki
spent most of his life
growing
SWEET PEAS
and
PETUNIAS
for an old lady.

... That's the kind of life
I try to
CELEBRATE.

yes,
we must have
secret places.

Not in order to hide
from the world,

but simply in order to
be with oneself
for a change —
to get to know oneself
a little,

because in the hurly-burly
of life
we can so easily become
strangers
to ourselves.

and when all the
wars are done,

a butterfly will still be
beautiful.

'GOD GAVE US OUR FACES,'
said Granny.

'WE GIVE OURSELVES OUR
expressions'

no words
HEAL
better than
the silent company
of a
FRIEND.

There is no harm in
sitting in an office
and
making money,

but sometimes you must
look out of the window
and look
at the changing light.

be like
water.
there's no stopping it.

no matter how tiny
the trickle,
it's going to get
Somewhere!

an old *Library* is a good place to get *Lost.*

if only the world had
no boundaries
and we could move
without hindrance,

without having to
produce passports ...
it really would be a
great beautiful world.

Loneliness can be
imposed on us,

but Solitude
is something we must seek.

I love to see
seeds sprouting
and coming up where
I have planted them,
even if they are only
chillies and beans.

all trees
are places of
POWER.

PADDLE YOUR OWN
CANOE
AND IF YOU
SINK,

YOU ONLY HAVE
YOURSELF
TO BLAME.

Some paths lead
nowhere,

others lead to a
spring of water.

the
birds will
locate water
even when our
taps run dry...

outer space
beckons...

we have degraded
     Planet Earth,
 so let's be up and
 see what we can do
to clutter up other worlds...

bye folks !

see you on Mars ...
or on Jupiter.

Courage, my friend.

May it last to the end.

for any beauty you
possess at sixteen,
be very grateful.

of the beauty
you have at sixty,
you may be proud.

it is your own
achievement.

A *fanatic* IS NEVER AT PEACE.

'Some call it laziness...
I call it deep thought.'

I think it was
Garfield the cat
who said that.

almost everyone
can do the
FIRST HALF
of anything.

only those
who do the
SECOND HALF
arrive.

when you find
a true friend,
and keep him,
you make friends
with yourself.

My greatest
friends have
been my readers...

BAD times are
   GOOD times to prepare for
      BETTER times.

winners
hang on...

when

losers

let go.

May you have
the wisdom to be
simple ...

From small beginnings,
all the world...

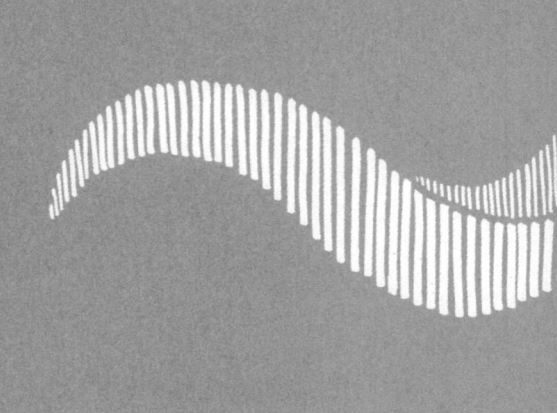

Reach for the sky).

Even if you
can't touch it,
you'll be an
arm's length nearer.

If you can
when you feel hurt,
the hurt is half cured.

BE HONEST,
GIVE YOUR OPINION FOR
WHAT IT'S WORTH;

THAT IS,
if you are asked for it.

What I valued,
I LOST;

What I gave,
I GAINED.

if you visit
your bean and lettuce merchant
every day,
you won't have to visit
your chemist.

hold on
to your dreams, and
don't let go...

Be guarded in your speech.

Don't talk too much.

Many words
      initiate
            many defeats.

if you want to travel

fast,

keep to the

old

roads.

What if you failed yesterday?

Today is not yesterday, is it?

WHEN TOO MUCH
WORK ACCUMMULATES,
TAKE A

holiday.

Life IS NOT SOMETHING TO PUT UP WITH,

BUT A *gift* TO BE ENJOYED WITH ZEST.

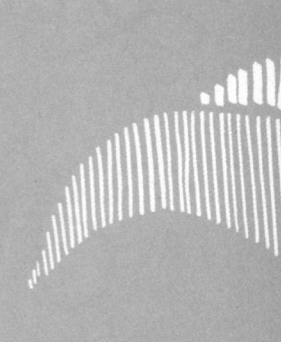

WHERE

all words

GO IN THE END—

OVER THE HILLS

AND FAR AWAY,

TO BE

lost forever.

Dormitory life seems to suit some people.

However, I've always wanted
my own space,
my own private room,

even if it's a small one.

the
tender green shoots
are the basic miracle
of life.

Do I contradict myself?

Very well, then, I contradict myself.

a room without
a window
is rather like a
prison cell.

MOST OF US GROW IN OUR
TEENS AND TWENTIES.

I THINK I GREW UP
WHEN I WAS TEN.

We come into this world
pure and innocent.

However, it doesn't take
long for us to be

tainted and corrupted
by the

warped civilization
that prevails around us.

A world controlled by
megalomaniacs, fanatics,
power-hungry individuals and
self-appointed
guardians
of our morals.

This is a book

of a few

words

and many

colours.

Destiny,
or the Great Librarian,
brought me to this hilltop.

Mother Hill
near Mother Ganga,
and here I have
spent my best days and
done my best work.

And here I stay,
until I have written
my last word.

About The Author

Ruskin Bond, one of India's best-loved writers, has written over 500 short stories, essays and novellas, and more than forty books for children. He received the Sahitya Akademi Award in 1992, the Padma Shri in 1999 and the Padma Bhushan in 2014.

Scan QR code to access the
Penguin Random House India website